POLITICALLY INCORRECT FEMALE CHAUVINIST JOKES ABOUT MEN

BY
JAMES BUFFINGTON

A POLITCISISFUN

HUMOR GOURMET DESSERT

COPY RIGHT 2008 BY JAMES BUFFINGTON
All rights reserved. No part of this book may be reproduced without permission of the author save brief passages for reviews praising the author and his works.

Cover design by James Buffington
Clipart courtesy of clipart.com, copyright 2008.
Used under license.

ISBN: 1438225334
EAN-13: 9781438225333.

INTRODUCTION

For years men have ridiculed the fairer sex. Now comes the time for revenge! Collected here are some of the best jokes about men ever told. So turn the page and dig in. And as you read be sure to glance over at your husband or boyfriend or co-worker and snicker. It'll keep 'em in their place and you know they deserve it.
Have fun, ladies!

"Of course I enjoyed you. "Didn't you hear me laughing?"

Post Coital Male Sex Practices

20% roll over and have cigarette.
2% washed up.
3% have a snack.
75% get dressed and go home

A man received a jigsaw puzzle from his wife for his birthday. It had all of 16 pieces. Eagerly he set up a card table in the basement and spent each night working on it for a week. Finally he bounded upstairs shouting, " Honey, I did it1 I finished the puzzle!"

"That's great, but it took you a whole week!"

"Yeah, and on the box it says " Two to four years!""

I went fishing with my boyfriend"

"Catch anything?"

"I'll know in a few days."

A shy guy had a new girlfriend. He wanted to have sex with her but was too afraid of rejection to ask. So one night he took her to a dark, secluded spot and they began necking. As they made out he opened his pants, took out his penis and placed it in her hand." "No thanks," she declined. "I don't smoke."

"I'm a lesbian because all the warm, caring, sensitive men have boyfriends."

A guy walks into a bar and sees an attractive woman sitting alone, drinking. He walks over to her and says, "Hi, my name is Bill. Could I buy you a drink?"
"I don't think so," replied the femme. "You see, I'm a lesbian."
"A lesbian? What's that?"
"Well," replied the woman, "You see that barmaid over there?" She nodded toward a cute blond server. "I'd like to take her to my place, strip off her clothes and make love to her."
"Golly, said the man, "I think I must be a lesbian, too!"

Two guys were walking along the beach on a bright and sunny day.
"Ouch!" cried one. "A crab just bit my toe!"
"Which one?"
"How should I know? Crabs look alike to me!"

Marcie, 8 months pregnant, was discussing delivery procedures with her doctor.
"Will my husband be allowed to be with me during the delivery?"
"Certainly. The father of the child is always welcome to attend the birth."
"I don't think that would be a good idea. He and my husband just don't get along."

Two girlfriends went to the opening of a new film together. The theater was crowded and people were packed into their seats like sardines.

"Hey," whispered the first, "the guy next to me is masturbating!"

"Well tell him to stop."

"I can't! He's using my hand!"

A cop is walking along the street and comes across a man jumping up and down.

'Anything wrong?" inquired the officer.

"No. I just took my medicine and forgot to shake the bottle."

Eros spelled backward is sore.

A girl feels pert
And fully chipper
When she meets up
With a friendly zipper

Why do gays make great parole officers?
They never let anyone finish a sentence.

How did the man know he had been sleepwalking?
He woke up in his own bed.

Clem complained to another farmhand that he was having trouble getting to sleep.
"Why don't you try counting sheep?" asked his friend.
So that night Clem gave it a try. " One, two, three, hello sweetheart, five…."

Then there was the guy who thought Taco Bell was the Mexican phone company.

A man had been picked for questioning by the police.

"You have quite a rap sheet," observed the detective with a furrowed brow. "Burglary. Armed robbery. Sexual assault. Sexual assault. Sexual assault…"

"Yes, sir. It took me a while to figure out what I do best."

What did the man say when he wrecked his car?

"That's the way the Mercedes Benz"

How is making love in a canoe like light beer?
They're both fucking close to water.

Cal came home from a business trip and found a used condom under the bed. "I know you've been cheating on me. Who was it? Was it my friend Lloyd?" he demanded of his wife."
"No," replied his wife.
"How about Bob?"
"No. I'm not talking!"
"How about Max? Was it Max?"
"What's the matter? Don't you think I have friends of my own?"

"But Mom! All the girls my age are wearing a training bra!"
"Shut up Gregory!"

"Would you like some ice cream, dear?" a man asked his wife.
"How hard is it?"
"About as hard as *you know what!*"
"In that case pour me some."

My husband made his money the old fashioned way. He inherited it."

A guy walks into the bar.
"What's your pleasure?" asks the barkeep.
"Balling. But I guess I'll have a martini."

Why are men so arrogant?
They think they're too good to go fuck themselves.

Love thy neighbor all through the day
But first make sure his wife's away

Why is a man like a dining room table? They both have an extra part that extends for entertaining.

"Your honor, I want a divorce, " said the wife to the judge. "My husband has been cheating on me."
"Do you have any evidence to support your claim of marital infidelity?"
"Yes, sir! Just yesterday I saw him walking down the street with the company of a blond. They went into a movie together."
"And who was this other woman?"
"I don't know. I never saw her before."
"Well, why didn't you go into the theater and find out?"
"The guy I was with had already seen the picture."

Why is beauty more important than brains for a woman?
A lot of men are stupid, but not many are blind

The Trials Of Man

When he's single the girls convince him he should be married.
When he's married his wife tells him he should have stayed single.
If he forgets to bring flowers she gets mad.
If he does bring flowers she gets suspicious.
If he comes home early she thinks he wants something
If he comes home late she thinks he's already had it.

Do men prefer sex with the lights on or off?
Yes.

Why is a woman like a remote control?
Because a man will randomly push the buttons until something happens.

Why do men pay more for car insurance than women?
Women don't get hand jobs while driving.

Bronson was talking with his buddy in a bar one cold and wintry night.
"My boss and I played golf in the snow yesterday."
"Really? Did you have to paint your balls?"
"Nah. We wore long johns."

"I've never had an affair, railed the husband. " Can you say the same?"
"Yes," replied the wife, " but not with such a straight face."

Bachelor

A mean spirited son of a bitch that's cheating some deserving woman out of her alimony.

Men are like computers. You don't appreciate them until they go down.

Anson was always going out by himself at night, leaving his wife to mind the house and kids. "Good night, mother of three!" he would call out cheerily.
Until the night she replied, "Good night, father of one."
Anson now stays home.

"How did you get your divorce?"
"It wasn't hard"

Adultery
Two wrong people doing the right thing

Why are taxi drivers such great lovers? They take as long as they can to get there.

A guy had been dating his new girl for several weeks and hadn't got anywhere. So he called her up.

"I'm tired of this waiting and fooling around. I'm coming over to your place and throw you on the floor and rip your clothes off…"

"Oh, no you're not!"

'… and then I'm going to screw you 'til your tongue hangs out…."

"Oh, no you're not!"

"… and I'm not going to even use a condom!"

"Oh yes you are!"

"My son Myron must be crazy," Myrtle said to her friend Sophie.
"Why do you say that?" asked Sophie.
"I heard him talking to his girlfriend on the phone and he said he hoped he'd be bald soon."

What animal has it's asshole halfway up it's back?
A police horse.

"No more credit," said the call girl to the john. "You're already into me for too much!"

Then there was the guy who was so ugly even his computer wouldn't go down on him.

"I believe in love at first sight. The first time I saw one I knew I'd love it!"

Louis retired to Florida with his much younger wife. Shortly after arriving he sought out a lawyer.

"I want to make a will," he explained. "I want to leave everything to my wife. My house, the investments, the cars, everything. But I have one condition. She must remarry within a year of my death."

"No problem," said the lawyer. "But why the condition?"

"I want at least one person to be sorry I died."

How do you know a man is good at cunnilingus?
Word of mouth.

Why don't women blink during foreplay?
No time.

Two avid girl watchers were at the ocean when a muscle bound beach bum swaggered down the shore with a bikini clad babe on each arm.
Said one to the other, "Would you look at the dolls on that boob!"

When you get married you find there are three stages in your sex life:
1. House sex. You make love in every room and on every piece of furniture.
2. Bedroom sex. After the kids are taken care of and sleeping you make love in the bedroom.
3. Hall sex. You pass each other in the hall and shout "Fuck you!"

Recreation
Making love to your husband even though you're pregnant.

1st guy: "What's the difference between a screw and a paper clip?"
2nd guy: "I don't know. I've never been clipped!"

Why did the man have sex with the lights on?
He forgot to close the car door.

Butch visited the local cathouse for an evening of fun. The madam fixed him up with three babes in the best suite in the joint and they had a grand time. When butch went to pay his bill the Madam said, "No charge. It's on the house."
The next week he returned and asked for the suite and the same three girls.
"That'll be a thousand dollars," replied the Madam.
"A thousand dollars! Last week it was free!"
"Last week was a pay per view webcast."

Why did the guy sew fur into his jockey shorts?
He wanted ball to ball carpeting.

Two guys were sitting at the bar. One of them thought he recognized a woman sitting at a table across the room.
"Hey", he asked, "isn't that Hortense?"
The second guy looked over. "She looks pretty relaxed to me."

What should a woman do with her asshole every morning?
Pack him a lunch and send him to work.

The couple was having a hung over breakfast after a wild all night party. "Honey," asked the husband, "was that you I made love to last night?"
"About what time?"

She was "Honey Child" in New Orleans
The hottest of the bunch
But on the old expense account
She was gas, repairs and lunch

What's the difference between a man and a light bulb?
The light bulb is brighter, but the man is easier to turn on.

A secretary walks into her boss's office first thing in the morning.

"Boss, I have good news and bad news for you."

'Just give me the good news," said her boss. "I don't want to start the day on a bad foot."

"You're not sterile."

"I'm yours for the asking. And I'm asking $500."

A traveling salesman was driving through the country when he felt the call of nature. He stopped by the road near a farmhouse next to a pumpkin patch. As a joke he cut off the top of a pumpkin, hollowed it out and took a dump in it. Then he put the whole thing back together and drove off on his way. On the return trip he came to the same field and felt a bit guilty about what he had done. So he pulled up to the farmhouse and knocked.

"Howdy," greeted the farmer who opened the door.

"Hi," returned the salesman. "I'm afraid I did something not very nice." And he proceeded to explain what he had done.

The farmer listened and when the salesman finished he moseyed to the phone and dialed.

"Hi, Sis," he said. "You were right about that pie."

How can you tell your husband is dead?
The sex is the same but the farts stop.

Why did the guy take two hits of LSD?
He wanted to go on a round trip.

How can you tell a man is well hung?
He turns blue and stops struggling.

Julie had just returned from a vacation in Rome and was chatting with her friend, Louise.
"Did you pick up any Italian," asked Louise.
"I sure did."
"What did you learn to say?"
"Oh, I didn't learn any words."

"I always have a grand and glorious feeling when a man makes love to me. But the grand comes first."

The bigger they are, the harder they ball

How can you spot a level headed man? He drools equally out of both sides of his mouth.

"This suit was a gift from my wife."
"Oh, yeah?"
"Yeah. I came home from work early one day and there it was on the back of a chair."

A man was lying on his death bed and called his wife over.

"Sophie, he whispered, "after I'm gone I don't want you to be lonely. I want you to find another man and get married."

"Okay, Seth. I will. I promise."

"One thing though. Promise me you won't let him wear any of my clothes."

"Don't worry. You're a 42 regular and he's a 48 long."

How can you tell a man is sexually aroused?
He has a pulse.

"I finally found Mr. Right. I just didn't know his first name would be "Always."

Guy: This is National Sex Week. Would you care to contribute?"
Gal: "Sorry, I gave at the office."

Then there was the cheater who got to first base with the barmaid and thrown out at home.

The newlyweds reached their bridal suite and began to undress.
"Honey," said the bride, "there's something I need to confess.
I used to be a topless dancer."
Oh, no!" exclaimed the groom. "I'd have just as soon married a prostitute!"
"Well, that's another thing…"

How does a bachelor keep his dinner warm?
Tin foil up the nose.

Joy, while working late one night
Turned off every office light
Her boss beside her whispered things
Of wedding bells and diamond rings
He pledged his love in burning phrase
And acted foolish many ways
When he left Joy laughed alone
And turned off her camera phone

How do you get a man to put the toilet seat down?
Cut off his cock.

They met, had a whirlwind romance and were married. As they disrobed in the bridal suite the groom asked, "Will I be the first to do this to you?"
"I don't know. What position do you want to try?"

What do you call a man with no arms?
Trustworthy.

Why do women fake orgasms?
Men fake foreplay.

A traveling saleswoman had her car break down in the country and ended up having to stay the night with a farmer, his wife and their son. Sure enough she had to spend the night in the same bed with the son. She was feeling horny and decided to get a little action going.

"How about trading sides with me?" she asked. "You roll over me and I'll roll over you and we'll be more comfortable."

So they did. She suggested this several times and each time they rolled around and nothing happened.

"You know," said the woman, "I don't think you really know what I want."

"The hell I don't," the son replied, " you want the whole damn bed, but you ain't a gonna get it!"

What does your asshole do when you have an orgasm?
He shouts out, "Hey, what's that buzzing in the bathroom?"

Why do men get married?
So they can stop holding their stomachs in.

How do you find a blind man in a nudist colony?
It ain't hard.

A man comes home from work early and finds his wife in the sack with another man.
"What the hell is going on here?" the husbanded demanded. "Who the hell are you?"
"That's a fair enough question," replied his wife. She turned to her lover. "What is your name?"

Why do penises have a big knob at the end?
To stop his hand from sliding off.

"My husband has never found a stranger in his closet. They were all his friends."

"Did he get fresh?"
"I'll say he did! I had to slap him three times before I gave in!"

How do you get your man to shout your name and gasp for breath?
Hold a pillow over his face.

"I know a guy who goes to bed every night at eight. He doesn't drink, curse, smoke or screw. He'll be six next week."

A woman was walking home one evening when a thug jumped out of the bushes. He grabbed her, ripped her clothes off and began to rape her.
"Help!" screamed the woman. "I'm being robbed!"
"You're not being robbed, lady," growled the thug. 'You're being screwed!"
"If you call this being screwed, I'm being robbed!"

How is a man like an ambulance?
They both make a lot of noise to let you know they're coming.

Mothers have Mother's Day.
Fathers have Father's Day.
Bachelors have Palm Sunday.

She: "If I go out with you will you promise not to fool around?"
He: "Yes, yes, I promise."
She: "Then I'm going out with Harry instead."

Two women were talking in the park one day.
"I take every precaution to avoid pregnancy," said the first.
"But I thought your husband had a vasectomy?"
'That's why.'

How do you get a man to listen to you?
Talk in your sleep.

Why do guys sleep better on their sides?
They have a kickstand.

Husband Swapping
A type of fourplay

Why did God give men cocks?
So women would talk to them.

Henpecked
A man who's afraid to tell his pregnant
wife that he's sterile.

How is a one night stand like a newsflash?
Both are short, unexpected and probably a disaster.

An old coot was talking to his doctor. "So," asked the doctor, "how's your sex life?"
"Well, two weeks ago I picked up a really swell 20 year old. Then last week I bedded a hot little grad student. And this weekend I seduced a nifty young barmaid."
"All these women!" exclaimed the doctor. "I hope you're taking precautions!"
"Sure!" returned the geezer. "I give them a phony name and number!"

"I knew a man with 5 pricks. His underwear fit like a glove."

Why do husbands close their eyes during sex?
They hate seeing their wives have a good time.

The would be Romeo approached the sweet young thing.
"How about joining me for a weekend in Vegas?" he asked hopefully.
"I'm afraid," she replied, "that my awareness of your proclivities in the esoteric aspects of sexual behavior precludes you from any such erotic confrontation."
"I don't get it."
"Exactly."

Why did the man always use a condom?
He learned from his parent's mistake.

A guy is walking along the beach and finds a bottle. When he opens it a genie flies out.
"I will grant you three wishes," promises the genie.
"Well, first, I'd like a bright red Mercedes."
Poof! The car appeared.
"Next I'd like a big mansion."
Poof! They were now in a luxurious mansion.
"Lastly, I'd like to be irresistible to women."
Poof! He became a box of chocolates.

Why do guys shake their cocks after they pee?
Because they can't train them to go *sniff*.

"Sorry, I'm not your type. I'm not inflatable."

What's the most useless thing on grandma?
Grandpa.

A guy and gal are on their first date together and go for a stroll in the woods. The guy is shy and mainly listens as the girl goes on about various subjects.

"Say," says the girl at last, "you don't talk much."

The guy whips out his cock and say, "I do my talking with this!"

"Sorry," says the girl, "I'm not into small talk."

What kind of man steals Viagra?
A hardened criminal

A wealthy man loses his job.
"We'll have to economize," he opines.
"If you could learn to clean and cook we could get rid of the housekeeper."
"And if you could learn to fuck we could get rid of the chauffeur."

What do pitchers and gigolos have in common?
Fast balls.

"I never made a man I didn't like"

"My favorite breakfast? Him and eggs."

What goes "Ha! Ha! Ha! Thump! Thump!"
A man laughing his balls off..

Men claim penises come in three different sizes. Large, medium and size doesn't matter.

Man: "I love you in the worst way!"
Woman: " Almost, but not quite."

The perfect male is long, dark and handsome.

A man's scariest horror movie? "Chain Saw Vasectomy."

"I'd love to fuck your brains out, but I see someone beat me to it."

A father receives his first letter from his son who had just entered the military.
"Dear Dad, I can't tell you where I am, but yesterday I shot a polar bear."
A few months go by and he gets another letter."
'Dear Dad, I can't tell you where I am but yesterday I slept with a hula girl."
A few more weeks go by.
"Dear Dad, I can't tell you where I am but the doctor says I shot have danced with the polar bear and shot the hula girl."

Then there was the butcher that backed into the meat grinder and got a little behind in his work.

What's the difference between a man and a cup of coffee?
A cup of coffee can keep you awake all night.

"It's true! Nice guys finish last!"

Mike and George, two guys in their late 70's, were talking about sex.

Mike said, "I think we should try oysters. I hear they put lead in your pencil."

"I don't know about you," answered George, "but I don't have any girls to write to."

Why is virginity like a balloon?
One prick and they're both gone.

Two drinking buddies hit the head at the local bar. One goes to a urinal, the other takes a stall.
"Hey, how come you always sit down to take a leak?" asks the one at the urinal.
"My doctor told me not to lift anything heavy."

What do German men call "Vaseline?"
Der Weinerslider.

Dogs are better than men. If a dog wants his balls licked he does it himself.

Man: "Am I the first to make love to you?"
Woman: "Of course! Why do you men always ask that same silly question?"

What's the difference between a man and a Rubik's Cube?
No matter how long you play with it the Rubik's cube will still be hard.

What's the difference between parsley and pussy?
Men won't eat parsley.

Why do women suffer from hemorrhoids rather than men?
Because when god made man he made the perfect asshole.

The best thing about being a woman? You can make a man come without calling him.

A feminist was giving a presentation at a university when a male voice called out from the back: "Don't you wish you were a man?"
"No. How about you?"

What's the difference between a clitoris and a golf ball?
Men will spend hours looking for a golf ball.

One guy was so ugly when he was born the doctor slapped his mother.

What's Wrong With Men

1. The belly button doesn't work
2. The tits don't give milk
3. His cock won't crow
4. His balls won't roll
5. His ass won't carry a thing.

Why do gays make lousy Santas?
Instead of filling your stockings they try them on.

A pervert at the airport was stricken by the stewardess checking boarding passes for his flight. When his turn in line came he suddenly exposed himself. "I'm sorry, sir. You'll have to show me your ticket, not your stub."

"My mother always told me to be good. Was I?"

A traveling salesman was going through the mountains when he felt nature call. Spying a shack ahead, he stopped and knocked on the door. A hillbilly opened the door.
'Howdy," he greeted.
"Hi," said the salesman, "I was wondering if I could use your bathroom?"
"Got a two seater right around back. Help yourself."
So the salesman went round back and opened the door. There on one of the seats was another hillbilly.
"C'mon in, Plenty of room." invited the second hillbilly.
So the salesman entered and dropped his drawers, and sat. As he did so the hillbilly got up. As he pulled up his pants some change fell out of his pocket and down the hole. The hillbilly pulled out a twenty dollar bill and dropped that down the hole as well.

"What did you do that for?" asked the startled salesman.
"You don't think I'm going down there for thirty five cents, do you?"

On what charges can you get a transvestite arrested?
Male fraud.

What's the difference between man and beer?
Beer comes in a can not in your mouth.

A young executive had been chasing a pretty co-worker for weeks, to no avail. Finally she gave in and agreed to have dinner with him.

Looking to get lucky that night he picked her up at her apartment and took her to a fancy French restaurant. When the waiter arrived he ordered a most expensive bottle wine. When the waiter took their orders he was shocked when the lass ordered half the items on the menu.

"Do you always eat this much?" he inquired with shock.

"No," she replied. "Only when I have my period."

Blessed are the pure for they shall inhibit the earth.

What's the difference between a battery and a man?
Batteries have a positive side.

What's the difference between a man and a lava lamp?
You turn on a lava lamp once and it goes up and down for hours.

What do you say to an impotent man?
"No hard feelings."

Two guys are walking down the street and spot a dog on a lawn licking his balls.
"I wish I could do that," said the first.
"You can try, but what if he bites?"

What do you call a woman with no asshole?
Divorced.

The Dean at the prestigious women's school called a young co-ed into his office.
"Your house mother tells me you smoke pot, snort coke, and have snuck almost every boy in town into your dorm room. Don't you know what good, clean fun is?"
'No. what good is it?"

What's the problem with oral sex?
The view.

Why do men prefer marrying virgins?
So they won't know what they're missing.

How is a man like a Slinky?
They're both amusing when they fall down stairs.

"Do you cheat on your husband?"
"Who else?"

What did the elephant say to the naked man?
"Cute, but can you eat peanuts with it?"

How many, attractive, caring, sensitive, honest, intelligent men does it take to satisfy a woman?
Both of them.

"Why don't you ever shout my name when you come?"
"I don't want to wake you up."

"I have a dog that growls, a parrot that curses, a fireplace that smokes, and a cat that stays out all night. Why on earth would I need a husband?"

What's the difference between medium and rare?
5 inches is medium, 10 inches is rare.

The newlyweds were in their honeymoon suite disrobing.
"Let me get my camera and take a picture of you naked," says the man.
"Why do you want to do that?" asks the bride.
"I want to remember you on this night forever."
"Okay," agrees the bride, "but then I want to take one of you."
"So you can remember me too?"
"So I can get it enlarged."

Why did the flasher refuse retirement?
He wanted to stick it out another year.

After dinner and a movie Melvin took Joan, his date, for a ride in the country. As they pulled down a secluded lane the car stopped.
"Oh, no," sighed Melvin. "Out of gas."
Joan smiled knowingly, reached inside her coat and pulled out a bottle.
"Well, " brightened Melvin. "What have we got here?"
"Gasoline."

Man
A device for turning fine wine into urine

Some guys like bondage. It's knot for everyone.

In the game of love we claim
There's only one reward.
It isn't how you play the game
It's how many times you've scored.

How is a man like a vacation?
Neither is ever long enough.

A guy was out with a blind date and as they drove to the restaurant he asked, "So what religion are you?"
"Actually, I'm a witch," she smiled back wickedly.
"So you can do magic? Show me"
"Sure". Then she whispered in his ear and he turned into a motel.

"The trouble with men is that they're so slow you want to scream or so fast you have to."

What's the difference between a man and a diaper?
You can change a diaper.

Why do men whistle while they sit on the toilet?
So they remember which end to wipe.

I met a fella who was willin'
Now I'm taking penicillin.

"Don't torture yourself. That's my job."

Then there was the bride that put a piece of wedding cake underneath her pillow for luck. The next morning she discovered that she woke up with a crumb.

What's the difference between a circus and a single bar?
At a circus the clowns don't talk.

The first grade class was playing "Guess The Animal." The first picture the teacher held up was that of a cat. "Ok, kids, what's this?"
"I know,' yelled one little boy. "It's a cat!"
"Very good!" She held up a picture of a dog. "And what is this?"
"It's a dog!' called out a little girl.
"That's right!" She held up a picture of a deer. No one answered. "I'll give you a hint. It's something your mommy calls your daddy around the house."
A little boy stood up and shouted, "That's a horny bastard!

Why do men with pierced cocks make the best husbands?
They've experienced pain and bought jewelry.

Why did the pervert cross the road?
He couldn't get his dick out of the chicken.

What's the difference between a penis and a paycheck?
It's always fun to blow a guy's paycheck.

A drunk going through the park came across a guy doing pushups. "Hey, buddy," said the drunk, "you lost your girl."

How many perverts does it take to screw in a light bulb?
One, but you have to go to the emergency room to get it taken out.

What's the difference between 69 and driving in a fog?
In a fog you can't see the asshole in front of you.

"I quit the porn business. I just didn't like some of the parts I was asked to play with."

What do a battery and an old man's balls have in common?
Dry cells.

"How many husbands have you had?"
"Counting my own?"

What's the difference between circumcision and divorce?
In divorce you get rid of the whole prick.

Welcome, welcome little stranger
You've made two hearts so glad
You took a big load off of Mother
And made room for dear old Dad.

Alimony
The screwing he gets for the screwing you got.

"I've never been so insulted in my whole life"
"What did the skunk do?"
"He drove me straight home! "

"Hey, Joe, your best friend is up at your place making love to your wife!"
"What?" and with that Joe dashed out. He came back twenty minutes later. "What are you talking about? I've never seen that guy before in my life."

What's the difference between a curtain and an erection?
The curtain doesn't come down until the performance is over.

"He reminded me of Don Juan. He's been dead for years."

"I pity Ruthie, Her fella doesn't drink smoke, swear or do drugs."
"Really?"
"Yeah, and he makes his own dresses."

What's the difference between a man and a jellybean?
Jellybeans come in many delicious flavors.

What's the difference between men and concrete?
Both take forever to get hard, but concrete only needs to get laid once.

"I put my husband in charge of sex and music. If I want his fucking advice, I'll whistle."

What do you get a man for his eighteenth birthday?
Bail.

It took tens of thousands of years for man to learn to walk on his hind legs, but his eyes still swing limb from limb.

If you want bread, sleep with a baker.

"Honey, why did you pull in here?" asked the sweet young thing as they drove round looking for some privacy. "There are so many nicer spots down the road.
"I know, but I believe in love at first site."

\

Three Stages Of A Man's Life

1. Tri-weekly
2. Try-weekly
3. Try-weakly

"Mommy, where were you when you met Daddy?"
"I was at a picnic."
"And was I with you?"
Not when I went, but you were when I came back."

Cats are better than men. When a cat sticks his butt in your face he doesn't expect you to lick it.

Why is sex like pot?
The quality depends on the quality of the pusher.

Why are hangovers better then men?
Hangovers are usually gone by lunchtime.

Motorcycles are better than men. They stay between your legs 'til you've had enough fun.

Why are Christmas trees better than men?
The balls are pretty to look at.

For years Bill and his wife had tried unsuccessfully to have a baby. His friends all suspected he was sterile.. Then one day he gleefully strode into the bar.

"Well, my wife just got back from the doctor and he says she's pregnant."

"Makes sense," commented one of his pals. "Nobody ever doubted her."

How can you tell a man from an ape? The ape peels the banana before eating it.

What's the difference between a man and a condom?
Condoms aren't thick and insensitive.

Benny and Marge were adjusting their clothes after a joust in the back seat of Benny's car.
"Sorry," said Benny. "If I knew you were a virgin I would have taken more time."
"Well, if I knew you had more time I would have taken off my panty hose."

Why do men give their dicks names?
They like being on a first name basis with the boss.

What do you do if a man asks you to turn over?
Laugh in his balls.

A guy walked into a pharmacy and asked for condoms.
"What color?" asked the pharmacist.
"It doesn't matter. Just give me an assortment.
So the druggist packed uo his order and the guy went on his way.
Almost a year later the guy returned to the pharmacy.
"Gimme a maternity bra." he said.
 "What bust?"
"One of the blue ones."

What three words do men hate the worst?
"Is it in?"

What three words do women hate most during sex?
"Honey, I'm home!"

How do you make a cock look bigger?
Buy smaller hens.

A wise woman makes her man feel like he's head of the house when he's really just chairman of the entertainment committee.

"Dad, what did you say to Mother when you proposed?
"I said, "The hell you say!" and we were married the next day."

Men are like cowpies. The older they are the easier they are to pick up.

What do you call a beautiful woman on the arm of a man?
A tattoo.

Why do men like big breast and tight pussies?
They have big mouths and small pricks.

What do you get when you cross a chicken with an onion?
A cock that will bring tears to your eyes.

"When it comes to giving he stops at nothing."

Why do men take showers instead of baths?
Because pissing in the bath is disgusting.

How To Impress A Man
Show up naked. Bring beer.

Every woman needs a husband. More things go wrong than you can blame on government.

A woman and a man were having sex in the middle of a dark forest. After about a while the man said, "I wish I'd have brought a flashlight."
"So do I. You've been eating grass for ten minutes."

What's the last thing a guy wants to hear in the men's room?
"Nice cock."

"My husband didn't leave a dime's worth of insurance."
Then were did you get that diamond ring?"
"Well, he left a thousand for a casket and five thousand for the stone. This is the stone."

Why do men masturbate?
It's sex with someone they love.

"His idea of a balanced meal is a beer in each hand."

Why do doctors spank babies so hard?
To knock the penises off the smart ones.

The reason men don't bring the boss home for dinner is that she's already there.

How can you tell a man has had an orgasm?
He's snoring.

"Do you wake up grouchy in the morning?"
"No, I let him sleep."

"My husband is like an angel. Always harping about something."

A woman was out shopping for her husband's birthday and stopped by a clothing store. The clerk was showing her some shirts.
"This would be perfect for the man about town," he beamed as he held up one bright number.
"How about something for the louse about the house?"

The delivery guys came with the new refrigerator.
"Be careful of my floors," cautioned the wife. "I just waxed!"
"Don't worry," grunted the first delivery guy. "We're wearing spiked shoes."

What do you get when you cross a man and a gorilla?
A dumb gorilla.

"Don't criticize my judgment. Look who I married."

"My husband really gets on my nerves! I'm so jittery I can't eat! I must have lost twenty pounds!"
"Then why don't you leave him?"
"As soon as I hit one fifteen."

Eternity
The time between when you come and he leaves.

"I think she married him because his uncle left him a million dollars."
"Nah. She would have married him no matter who left him the million."

Wife: "But dear, this isn't our baby!"
Husband: "Hush. It's a better carriage."

Loser
A guy who tries to get laid at a family reunion.

"My husband is a light eater. As soon as it's light out he starts eating."

"My ex paid so little attention do me that if I died he wouldn't be able to identify the body."

What do a toilet, a clitoris and an anniversary have in common?
Men miss them all.

Little girl: "Mommy, why can a woman have only one husband?"
Mommy, "The law protects those who can't protect themselves."

How many men does it take to screw in a light bulb?
One. He sticks it in the socket and waits for the world to revolve around him.

"If his ship came in he'd be too lazy to unload the boat."

A guy is spending the night in a cheap motel. He calls the front desk.
"Hey, I gotta leak in my sink!"
"Go ahead. Everyone else does."

What is the ideal weight for a man?
Three pounds, including the urn.

"How's your new boyfriend? Is he a steady guy?"
"He's so steady he's practically motionless."

How do you stop a man from drowning?
Shoot him before he hits the water.

"That's my side of the story. Now let me tell you his."

"I just hired my husband a new secretary."
"Blonde, brunette or redhead?"
"Bald."

Girls tend to marry men that remind them of their fathers. That's why mothers cry at weddings.

What do you call ten men skydiving?
Skeet.

If you have half a mind to get married, do it. That's all it takes.

Wedding Ring
A tourniquet worn around the finger to cut off circulation

"He can stay longer in an hour than most people do in a week."

"If you have the hose I have the garden."

"Men aren't sex addicts. They have restless groin syndrome."

"You can always tell my husband, but you can't tell him much."

What should you do if your husband wants you to be more affectionate? Get a couple of boyfriends.

Sophie's husband passed away. The funeral director asked her, "Do you want him buried or cremated?" "Why take chances? Do both!"

"Save your breath. You'll need it to blow up your date."

If your husband, your lawyer and your mother in law are trapped in a burning building, what do you do?
Take in a movie.

Why do little boys whine?
They're practicing to be men.

What's the difference between a husband and a boyfriend?
Forty five minutes.

What's the difference between a husband and a boyfriend?
About thirty five pounds.

What should you do if you see your husband staggering around outside the house?
Reload.

What's the difference between love and insanity?
Insanity is forever.

Give a man an inch and he thinks he's a ruler.

"Not only did he lie about the size of his yacht he made me do most of the rowing!"

"I'll admit I'm right if you'll admit you're wrong!"

"If it has tires or testicles it's a problem."

"My husband has expressive compulsive disorder."

\

"It's better to have loved and lost than never to have lost at all."

"All men are animals, but some make better pets."

"Sorry, I don't date outside my species."

"My sign? Do not enter!"

"Men suffer from Venus envy."

"I love married life. I hate shopping with my own money."

How many men does it take to lube your car?
One, if you hit him right.

How can you tell a man is an intellectual?
His lips don't move when he reads.

What's the difference between a blue eyed man and a brown eyed man?
The blue eyed man is a quart low.

Why did the man return his necktie?
It was too tight.

What's the lightest thing in the world?
A penis. Even a thought can raise it.

What's the surest form of birth control?
Laughter.

This guy gets drunk and on a lark goes into a tattoo parlor. In a stupor he has them tattoo "I love you" on his cock. The next night he and his wife are making love when she sees it and cries, "I cook for you! I clean for you! now you're trying to put words in my mouth!"

Then there was the man who confused Vaseline with putty.
All his windows fell out.

A man gives his son twenty bucks on his 16th birthday and told him to go down to the local cathouse for his first piece. As he's on his way he runs into his granny. She asks him where he's going and he tells her. Granny tells him to save his money, takes him back to her cottage and deflowers him.

When the boy gets home Dad asks, "Well, son how was it?"

"Great! I got laid and saved the twenty bucks!"

"How did you do that?"

"I ran into granny and she took care of me for nothing!"

"What! You mean you screwed my mother?"

"Why not? You screw mine."

A business man asks his wife one day, "If I were disfigured would you still love me?"
Of course, dear. I'll always love you."
"How about if I lost my virility and couldn't make love anymore"
"Sweetie, relax. I'll always love you."
"What about if I lost my job as a corporate vice president and didn't make 6 figures anymore?"
"I'll always love you, honey. I'd miss you, but I'd love you."

What's worse than an out of tune piano? An organ that goes flat in the middle of the night.

A construction worker comes home early and finds another guy in bed with his wife. Furious, he hits the other man over the head with a wrench and knocks him unconscious.

When the man regains consciousness he finds he's naked in the garage with his cock locked in a vise. On the workbench next to him is a dull, rusty hacksaw.

"Please, mister, don't cut it off!" pleads the cheater."

Don't worry, I won't," promises the construction worker. "I'm going to set the garage on fire."

There's a new morning after pill for men.
It changes his blood type.

What do you call a man who weeps
while he masturbates?
A tearjerker.

Do men prefer pantyhose or bare legs?
They prefer something in between.

Egghead.
What Mrs. Dumpty game Humpty.

"My ex is a hobosexual. One bum fuck."

A fellow visits a friend in Australia who lives in the outback. The Australian says he came at a good time. They're having a dance that night.
"Hey," says the visitor, I don't see a girl in this whole town. How are you having a dance?"
"We show up an hour early at the saloon and pick out a sheep."
"Well, I can see that," begrudges the visitor, "but why an hour early?"
"Cripes, mate! You wouldn't want to get stuck with an ugly one!"

Judge Jones was nearing retirement, which had him in a really bad mood. That day a drunk was brought before him. He had his license revoked years earlier, but still continued driving and getting picked up on DWIs.
"Just why is it," railed the judge, "That in the previous 15 years you've appeared before me almost two dozen times?"
"Well, judge, it's not my fault you've never been promoted."

Then there was the man who was acquitted of rape due to temporary insanity.
Men don't have enough blood to run two heads at once.

The lawyer was uneasy. His millionaire client was up on a murder charge and things looked grim. Desperate, he secretly contacted a poor lady juror with no husband and three hungry mouths to feed. He offered her a million dollars if she could get her client found guilty of second degree manslaughter instead. She agreed. After the trial the jury met for a nerve racking week, finally bringing in the second degree manslaughter verdict. A couple days later the lawyer went to the lady's house with $1,000,000 cash. "Thanks for you're hard work," said the lawyer. "How'd you do it?"
"It wasn't easy getting that verdict. Those other folk thought he was innocent."

Men laugh three times at jokes.
Once when you tell it.
Once when you explain it.
Once when they understand it.

A guy goes to see a psychiatrist.
"Doc, all I can think about all day long is making love to a horse. I can't get the thought out of my mind!"
"I see," replied the shrink. "And would that be a stallion or a mare?"
"A mare. What you think I am? Queer?"

A woman comes home and shows her husband several new bras she purchased.
"Why'd you bother?" he growled. "You don't have anything to put in them."
"I iron you're shorts, don't I?"

What does a man have in his pants that a woman doesn't want in her face? Wrinkles.

What's the difference between an old man and a penis?
When you hold a penis the wrinkles disappear.

Then there was the guy who turned to drink when his woman left him.
He got his dick caught in the neck of the bottle.

Why did the man name his dog "Herpes?
It wouldn't heel.

Then there was the nervous bank robber who went up to the teller shouted, "Ok, mothersticker! This is a fuck up!"

What's the cheapest way to bury a man?
Flush.

What do you do if a man is too big for his casket?
Give him an enema and put him in a shoebox.

If whiskey makes you frisky and gin makes you grin, what makes you pregnant?
Two highballs and a squirt.

Six year old Suzie was playing with the boy next door when he dropped his drawers, exposed himself and said, "I have something you don't got!"
Crying, she ran into the house and told her mother what had happened.
The next day she was again playing with the boy when he dropped his drawers again.
"So what?" said Susie as she dropped hers. "I have one of these and Mommy says with one of these I can get all of those I want!"

A woman got divorced and remarried shortly thereafter. As luck would have it she and her new love were invited to a party where her ex was also in attendance.

Seeking a suitable opportunity the ex caught his wife alone and asked, "So how does your guy like having used merchandise?"

"Just fine. Especially when he gets past the used part.

"Son, I want you to grow up to be a gentleman.

"But dad, I don't want to be a gentleman. I want to be like you!"

What's the coldest part of an Eskimo?
His balls. They're two below.

A sixteen year old boy comes home and brags to his dad, "Pop, I just got laid for the first time."
"Great! How was it?"
"Well, it sure made my asshole sore!"

A guy is walking down the beach and comes upon an old oil lamp. He rubs it and a genie appears. The genie tells him that he can have two wishes. "Well,' says the guy, "I want to be hard all the time and get all the ass I want." And so the genie turned him into a toilet seat.

A male porn star decided he needed new representation and set up an appointment with an agent.
"Do you have an 8' by 10'?" asked the agent?
"If I had an 8' by 10' I wouldn't need an agent."

Wet Dreams
Coming unscrewed

A guy walks into a whorehouse and says "I want a girl."
"Harry, grease up Beth!," the madam calls into the back, then the john, "That'll be a hundred bucks."
"Oh, that's too much!"
"Harry. Grease up Mabel! That'll be fifty bucks."
"Oh, that's too much."
"Harry, grease up Daisy. That'll be twenty five bucks."\
"I haven't got twenty five bucks."
"How much do you have?"
"Two bucks."
"Harry, grease up!"

Why did the man show up at the Halloween party naked and covered with whipped cream?
"He went as a wet dream."

"Dad, I got an "A" in spelling!"
"You dummy! There ain't no "a" in "spelling!""

Bachelor
A man who prefers to ball without the chain.

How do men most abuse their wives?
They stay married to them.

How can you tell a man is a connoisseur?
He knows what wine goes best with an enema.

How do men make up for their lack of good looks?
With their stupidity.

Why do men have blank bumper stickers?
They don't want to get involved.

What do you call a woman who's happily married?
Deaf, dumb and blind.

Male Code Of Honor
Never lie, cheat or steal.
Unnecessarily

It was the big game between Harvard and Yale. Two alumni, one from each school, and who were terrible rivals happened to run across one another in the men's room. As they finished the Harvard man heads for the sink while the Yale man zips and heads for the door.
"At Harvard they teach us to wash after urinating."
"At Yale they teach us not to piss on our hands."

What do you sit on that begins with "d" and ends with "k?"
A dock.

"Daddy, why do you write so slow?"
"I have to. I'm a slow reader."

Husband: "I think our son got his brains from me."
Wife: "He must have. I still have mine."

A wife comes home from the Saturday grocery shopping and asks her husband, "Where's the newspaper"
"Oh, I wrapped the garbage in it and threw out."
"I wanted to see it!"
"Not much to see. Just some coffee grounds and orange rinds."

Why do so many men remain single?
Like father, like son.

"Bart's the perfect man. He has his mother's looks and his father's money."

Then there was the woman who refused his proposal for religious reasons.
He was broke and she worshipped money.

Nothing gives a man
More of a chill
Then to have his honey ask,
"Have you made out your will?"

How can you tell what a man had for dinner?
Look at his shirt.

What's the leading cause of spontaneous combustion?
Fat men in corduroys.

Where is a man guaranteed to get a date?
On his tombstone.

Teacher: "Can you give me an example of how heat expands things and cold contracts them?"
Male student: "Well the days are longer in the summer nd colder in the winter."

Husband
A human gimme pig

When do men start to look good?
Two minutes before closing.

Gentleman

A man who grinds his cigarette into the carpet so it won't burn a hole.

How can you tell a man has something on his mind?
He's wearing a hat.

What's the worst advice you can give a man?
Be yourself.

What's the highest amongst men? Their I.Q.s or their golf scores?
Their weight.

What happened when the man called the suicide hotline?
They told him it would be a good idea.

How can you tell a well bred man? He takes his shoes off before putting his feet on your coffee table.

"I'd give anything to have a baby," opined Margie, "but no matter what we try I can't conceive."
"Have you tried a faith healer?" asked her friend Betty."
"Yes, we went, but it didn't do any good."
"Silly girl. Next time go alone."

"Remember how I complained I wasn't getting enough sex? Well now I'm getting all I want."
"Oh? Is it a new pill of some kind?"
"No. My husband's company sent him in the road."

A general and an admiral were sitting together in a bar when a corporal came in with a beautiful babe on his arm. The general sent a note to the corporal: "I believe I met you at the academy and the admiral thinks he met you at Michigan State. Please come over and straighten us out."
The corporal sent a note back: "I have never been to the academy, not to Michigan State. I have, however, attended taxidermy school and I'm mounting this bird myself."

1st guy: A divorce isn't the end of the world. There are plenty of other fish in the sea. You'll see."
2nd guy: "Maybe, but this one took all my bait."

1st guy: " My wife ran off with my golfing buddy."
2nd guy: "Don't worry. You'll soon replace her."
1st guy: "Yeah, but not him. He's the only one at the club I can beat."

Two college buddies are drinking at the campus brewery. Finally one of them passes out and keels over on the floor. "That's what I like about Bob. He knows when to quit."

"I have a foot fetish. I love anyone with twelve inches."

"I like a man who's like the stock market. Up and down and up and down…."

A guy goes to get on a crowded bus. "Is the ark full," he asks the driver. "No. we need one more jackass."

A guy dashes into the men's room, rushes to the urinal, unzips his fly, unleashes his twelve incher and begins to unload. "I just made it," he sighs to the guy next to him."
"Gee, I wish you'd make me one"

"I insured my cock for $100,000."
"What did you do with the money?"

1st secretary: "When did you first realize you were in love with the boss?"
2nd secretary: "The day he asked me to check his bank balance."

"If my ex misses an alimony payment do I have to repossess him?"

What's 18 inches long and hangs in front of an asshole?
A man's tie.

A one hundred and five year old man and his ninety eight year old wife checked into their hotel room. "I think I'll lay down a bit," said the man. "Okay," said his wife, "I'm going down to play the slots." And with that she left. Three hours later she returned and found her husband in the arms of a sexy young hooker. With a scream she picked him up and threw him out the window.

Horrified, the hooker screamed, "But we're on the twenty fifth floor!"

"At his age, if he can screw, he can fly!"

There's a new game called "Ovarian Roulette." You get to pick from six guys. Five have vasectomies.

"You can marry more money in five minutes than you can earn in a lifetime."

A guy says to his wife, "Dear, you haven't nagged me all evening. Is there someone else?"

Why are there no father in law jokes?

Men need wives. Otherwise they might go through their whole lives thinking they have no faults at all.

Marriage
A war in which you sleep with the enemy.

What does a male have that proves he's a man?
His birth certificate.

"We have an open marriage. He opens the mail and I open his wallet."

"Why do you want a divorce," asked the judge.
"I complained we didn't have enough outside interests. He bought me a lawn mower."

"Thanks! It's been a business doing pleasure with you!"

Jim has been collecting jokes and humor for over thirty years. Having graduated Cleveland State in 1974, he spent the next 23 years in a variety of positions while pursuing the lifestyle of a bridge bum. Currently Jim operates the popular gift and t-shirt site, politicsisfun.com. He was finally corralled by his wife, Gail, in 1997. They have 3 children, 2 of which are autistic. Proceeds from this book and other endeavors are for their future. They currently reside in Northeast Ohio. The family is owned by 2 cats, Callie and The Gray, who attend to all their spiritual needs. Jim is available for hire for humor and writing projects and may be reached at jimbuf2000@gmail.com

Look for all these Politicsisfun.com books coming soon:

Politically Incorrect Blond, Brunette And Redhead Jokes.
Little Willie's Rhymes and Crimes
Autistic Loves: Vignettes Of Joy
2008 T-Shirt Wit And Wisdom
Success Secrets Of The Illuminati
Politically Incorrect Female Chauvinist Jokes About Men

All will be exclusively available through Amazon.com

Search on the author's name, James Buffington, For these and future titles.

Visit our website, Politicsisfun.com. We have a wide variety of clothing and gift items in our gift shop. We have thousands of unique and amusing designs, all available only through Politicsisfun.com.

It's a great place for you to do all your gift buying! And get something smart for your self as well!

Printed in Great Britain
by Amazon